GRAFTED IN, BECOMING FAMILY

A NEW CREATION

by Kayla Jarmon

Grafted In, Becoming Family: A New Creation by Kayla Jarmon
Published by Tamarisk Tree Publishing

www.KaylaJarmon.com

The text of this book is set in Kopius and Broadsheet

Book formatting and cover design by The jCo Creative
Cover illustration by Piper Mirú © 2021

Printed in the U.SA.

For information about special discounts available for bulk purchases, sales promotions, fund-raising and educational needs, contact admin@kaylajarmon.com

First Edition

ISBN: 978-1-948706-07-0

Dedication

There's no better one to dedicate this book to than to God. He is the author of my faith and he completes it. If not for him drawing me to himself I wouldn't be grafted into his forever family. I am his child because of his unending love.

He breathed life into my being as he gave me life in Christ and brought forth a new creation in me. I was born again as John chapter three discusses. Jesus told of this new birth when he talked with Nicodemus, a leader in Israel. And that's what transpired with me when I was born into God's family. The old had gone and the new had come—as I accepted Christ as my Lord and Savior. Christ's finished work on the cross and his rising from death completes the saving grace of God for all who will receive God's gift.

Grafted In, Becoming Family is a series that starts with my salvation story and will continue to navigate through life's journey, this side of heaven. In the same way a newborn learns to walk, eat, play, work and grow to adulthood, we Christians continue to grow and mature in our walk with God.

God reveals himself to us, along the way. The Scriptures reveal that there's a Spiritual war transpiring in this world, and within God's children. As we live on this side of heaven we're not absent from the presence of sin—sin in others, sin in the Church and the sin nature within ourselves. Before we come to Christ we are aware of sin, but we perceive it as "right and wrong" based off of our personal convictions and experiences at the time. When we turn to God he illuminates what is good and what is evil because God is the source of good. Without him we're all left to our own assumptions, predispositions and judgement and they often change on a dime.

The process of discovering God, listening and following him is what this series is about and it happens as we walk with him; A process called sanctification. This series will highlight what that looks like as believers walk with God, within their families, with each other, in the Church and in the world. It will show the good, bad and ugly of that process. It's a walk where, like a baby stumbles with growth, we too stumble in our walks. But as we pursue God and he walks with us, we will be changed. We will be transformed to reflect his love to all around us. There's a wrestling that happens as we're transformed because of the sin nature that cries out for its way. We must decide with each struggle, with each impasse we must decide. What is God's will here, in this moment? And we must decide.

God is after the thought and intent of the heart. He is called our father for a reason. He is near, he cares, he reveals and he loves us. A closer walk with him is what he desires and what we can achieve with him leading and refining us—from the inside out.

Therefore, I dedicate this book and this series to him. He will do his work, as you read the series. The book ends with a cliffhanger. The second book will pick up where book one stops. So be prepared to read book two because the walk with Christ continues. Sanctification is an ongoing work in our lives, until we see him face to face and we'll know as we are known!

My prayer for all who read this book/series:

Father, I pray that all who read this book and series will either come to know you through Christ our risen Lord, and/or continue to grow in their walk with you, every day of their lives—a moment at a time. And that you, Father, will use my examples, the good, bad and ugly of them, to shine forth your redeeming work. And as you do that, that each person who reads will grow and be touched by you, God, through what you've done in and through me. Then your Scriptures in 1Corinthians 1:1-3 will be manifested and lived out—in and through me and them. I ask these things in Christ's name, for your glory, Father God, and for their good. Amen.

Special Thanks

My Husband, Don: This book would not exist if you hadn't thought of my creating it as a book series. I'll never forget being in the car and where we were at when you suggested it. My heart leapt at the thought! I immediately wanted my laptop! What a wonderful idea that you spoke forth. I pray God breathes his Spirit within the pages of this series and that all readers will indeed be grafted into his forever family and/or grow immensely—as they pursue knowing their God.

Ryan and Sarah Jarmon: I LOVE the work you do, from book cover formatting to all the interior formatting! This one was a little tougher to think through but you did it—and I LOVE it! The care that you exert in your creativity blows me away. Others will greatly benefit from JCO Creative as you continue to grow.

Ann Clapp: My fabulous editor! You are a forever friend and I so appreciate you!

My Family: Thanks to all of you. You help me to dream and to write. Every day I'm astounded with all of you. You spark my creativity and cause me to write. Then in turn you are my sounding board, on which I can depend. Many of you have art, illustrations, books, films, documentaries and songs within you... just waiting to come forth. Continue being you because you're a blessing to all around you! I love you more than you know and I'm thankful for you!

My Friends: All my friends are supportive and great encouragers. I'm so thankful that God has blessed me with true friends! I love you all!

About Grafted In

Grafted in was originally to be a T.V. series to show what true sanctification looks like. I wrote, directed and produced a proof of concept to see how it would do. Somehow a Christian broadcast network saw it and approached us about airing it. They would waive the fee to air it each week and help us with marketing and would drive people to our website. However, because they were a nonprofit company they could not pay for the production. They invited us to their annual convention as their guest, and we decided to go.

While there, I was in one of their offered seminars. One of the writers of the Waltons TV show was in the same class as well. He asked a question that was on my heart and, in my opinion, he didn't get a helpful answer. At that point I thought, *if he can't figure this out, how can little ole me figure it out?* We decided to put on the brakes with our films and continue with business promos, events, etc.

Flash forward a few years and God turned my heart toward writing books. One evening I was in the car with my husband and he asked, "Why don't you write *Grafted In* as a book series?" I couldn't believe it! I immediately thought, *that's a good idea! I wish I had my laptop with me right now!*

That's how it has come to you in book form. However, I wrote the original proof of concept as a fictional series, but decided to go a different direction with the book series... at least the first book. I thought, *why should I reinvent the wheel? I should share my story, what God has done in my life. That's how we're called to live.* It made total sense to me. Then there's no question to the accuracy of the subject matter. It's true and it happened in my life.

God is good and he draws us to himself for salvation. How we respond to that calling matters. The same holds true for us after we accept salvation; How we respond to God *in* our walk matters, too. And this is the theme of the series, how we respond and interact with God, as he works in our lives.

It's called sanctification.

This is my salvation story. At least book one is. And parts of my sanctification thread will remain throughout the series. It will be based on a true story. There's something raw with sharing this so openly to the world. God tells us in 1 Corinthians (and other places) that we're to share what he has done in our lives. After writing book one, *A New Creation*, I sought the Lord to see if I should indeed move forward with it. If he wanted me to, I could go a different direction with it or not publish it at all. One Saturday night, I really sought him on it. I needed to know. The next morning I was at church and it took me a second to put together that he was answering my question.

We began our worship with singing. However, the songs that we sang were not our typical style. The second one was one of my favorite songs from the beginning of my salvation and throughout my walk, "Blessed Assurance". Tears welled as I felt God's love and loved on him in return. Then the next song we sang was my Great Grandmother's favorite song, "How Great Thou Art". What?! I never met her because she died before I was born. But after salvation I told my mother how much I loved that song and she told me it was one of her mother's favorite songs too. This morning's worship was proving to be extra special for me. They usually didn't sing older songs/hymns like this. They would insert them here and there... but this particular morning there were two of them, back to back. And they were special ones to me. I felt God's love embracing me and I felt warm and cozy with him. And then the next song was the song I walked the aisle of the church to in proclamation of my accepting Christ as my savior. It was "Just as I Am".

How special was this? I felt so loved by God as he was surrounding me with memories of our journey together. And then it hit me. "Wait! You're answering my prayer!" Never before had worship enveloped my walk as this one did. My mother's side of the family had prayed for their future generations and "How Great Thou Art" was a favorite of her mother's. "Just As I Am" was the song I walked to the front of the church declaring my salvation. And "Blessed Assurance" was my staple song from the beginning of my walk with Christ.

God was replaying my story with him, i.e., our story. In his sovereignty he had the worship team pick those songs. He knew I'd be seeking him about sharing my story with the world. And my story was wrapped up in that morning's worship. He calls us to share what he has done in our lives. This book and series will do that very thing. The songs were reminding me of his workings in my life. Even going back to family I had never met praying for my salvation, and this book discusses that very thing. I said, "I get it God. Thank you," as tears began flowing down my cheeks. It was my story with him. It *is* my story with him. And I would share it.

The book you are holding is the first book of the series. *Grafted In, Becoming Family: A New Creation* is just one story of how God works to draw people to himself. God wants a family and he had family on his heart from the beginning of creation. He created Adam and Eve to be family. Satan hates family and tries to destroy it wherever he can. He started with Adam and Eve and because of their sin, which all mankind inherited, he attacks us individually, especially where it relates to family.

That's the struggle we all have. And that's why Christ came to earth. He is the way out of the struggle. He is the way back to being in God's family. He is the provision, *the gift* from God. He, as our Father, provided the answer to our problem. He reversed the situation for all who would come to him. His call goes out to all. Will you listen? Will you come to him?

This series reveals how God enters into the struggle with his children. How we respond to God is always a pivotal place in life. Will we come to him as the way back to his family? If yes, then we are established as his child through Christ. When we become his child we have eternal life but that life begins now, on this side of heaven. But while here, how do we live this side of heaven with him? We are a new creation as a child of God. The old is gone and the new has come.

All mankind is born through a mother and a father. There's no other way to get here except through that designed way. In that same way, there's no other way to get to heaven but through being born through the Spirit of God given to us by Christ, God's way back to himself—as you're born into his family. Through his gift of Christ, you become a new creation and are then grafted into God's family. You become part of God's family. *Grafted In, Becoming Family: A New Creation* is the first in the series that reveals just *some* of God's workings before you.

It's my prayer that God will give you eyes to see him, ears to hear him, and a heart to respond to him and enter into his family. Then my prayer continues for you, that you will always have eyes looking to him and ears listening and responding to his voice as you live a life that shows his love to the world. For that is what God wants, *family.*

Contents

A Note from the Author

The following story is based on events that actually unfolded in my life. The road to my salvation is a long one. Varied are the colors and shapes on my life's canvas. Some colors are dark with sharp, fragmented shapes. However, God uses all things to bring us to himself. The names have been changed here, but the re-created conversations, struggles, and conversion are true—to the best of my ability to convey.

To remain true to the veracity of the story, the darkness must be seen as it is—dark. In chapter 11, the language in the conversation that transpired was extremely harsh. I refrained from writing the obscenities that were spewed at me. Instead, I made substitutions for them. Now that I'm years into my own sanctification, I desire to clean up what transpired. It's hard to replay and to write the words that were spoken to me or to inflict them upon my readers. Therefore, context will lead the reader as he/she reads the substitutions for the omitted obscenities. Darkness is wrong, and it feels wrong. And the depth of darkness is rightly measured when the light has exposed it.

A New Creation is book one in this series. The series will highlight the nature and walk of a child of God and what that walk looks like, i.e., the internal struggles as well as the external ones. Book one deals with the Lord leading and drawing me to salvation and how the enemy tries to thwart that. The rest of the series reveals how a child of God progresses and navigates their new life in Christ in this world... the good, the bad, and the ugly of it. My prayer is that God's mercy will find its place in your heart and if you don't already know him, that you'll run to him. And if you do know him, I pray that you'll grow more in love with him and in your compassion for others.

Chapter 1

How Did I Get Here?

Went home, I don't feel well. That's all I wrote on the legal pad. That's all I could manage to write. My handwriting betrayed what I wanted to conceal—my disturbance of peace. A few hours ago, I woke to the blackness of the night, sitting up abruptly. The blue-gray moonlight bounced off the mirror, illuminating the room more brightly than usual. I could make out his body next to mine. His heavy breathing indicated that he was down for the count. His shoes on the floor revealed his walking out of them on the way to bed. His shirt was hanging half off the chair where he flung it, and his pants were crumpled on the floor, indicating they were the last thing he stepped out of before hitting the bed. He was face down with one leg and hand dangling off the side of the bed.

My heart was pounding... I woke with an alarming inclination to get up and go home. It was as if someone were urging me to leave. I reasoned with myself, it'd be crazy for you to get up and leave at this hour. Go back to sleep... you can leave in the morning. I agreed with this reasoning and lay back down to get more sleep.

When my eyes opened again, the urgency returned. "Leave!" is all it said. That's when I knew our plans for the day would be interrupted. This urgency demanded my departure... I had to leave. But why, I couldn't tell you. In fact, that was the question to answer. I knew things needed to change.

I'd been wrestling with that notion for months. I wrote my note for Brad and left it on the table, then fumbled for my keys and left. Once inside my car, I couldn't get home fast enough.

I felt desperate, and I didn't know why. As I drove, I noticed what a beautiful day it was. I wanted to embrace it. I wanted to fully enjoy the crispness it held—but I couldn't. Others passed me, and I passed others, and all were seemingly able to freely enjoy it except me. Probing thoughts and emotions brought an acute awareness of my surroundings and seemed to slow things down for their contemplation. I passed families playing in their yards. I wanted their ability to enjoy this day, and I wanted what they seemed to possess. A dense fog was enveloping my being. My mind was syncing with my heart in search of answers. Questions were swirling, and I knew they'd be relentless for answers. But for now, clarity was shrouded in this insidious, invasive fog.

Early this morning, Brad left to play golf. How he can party so hard and get up so early to play golf is beyond me. Upon his return, we were supposed to go enjoy the beautiful afternoon and evening by dining and hanging out with friends. We had planned a picture-perfect day. I would leisurely awaken and lounge around the house. Early afternoon, I would be ready to go to our favorite outside-dining restaurant. Then we'd pursue the evening with fun entertainment. But that was now derailed, and my note would reveal it to him soon enough.

I knew he'd call when he saw the note—I was sure of it. Although I didn't want him to call—not now, and not this afternoon but, I knew he would. I wanted to be alone to figure this out, but he'd call. The urgency that prompted my quick exit was an intruder, to be sure. Yet there was something that felt familiar about it, too. When abruptly awakening to it in the middle of the night the reasoning I asserted caused it to relent. But with the morning light—it returned. Whether friend or foe, it was upon me in full force. It was surreal, and yet it connected with me, and nothing less than my leaving would appease it. And so I left. And I needed to be alone to figure things out.

Eventually, Brad did call, and his first words were, "Nicole, what's wrong?"

I wondered why he thought something was wrong, so I asked, "Why do you think something's wrong?"

"I could tell by your handwriting that something's wrong."

I knew my handwriting would betray me. The urgency didn't care how neat my writing was... it simply pushed me to leave. I said, "I don't know what's wrong. I just needed to come home, that's all. So, I did."

He said, "But we had our afternoon planned. I was looking forward to it, weren't you?"

"Yes." I went on, "But when I woke up this morning, I knew I needed to come home."

He paused, then said, "I know what's wrong with you." He did? I was glad to hear someone knew. He continued, "You know things can't continue as they are." Boy, I knew this was truth! I had been contemplating that truth for months, but how did he know? He continued, "You know we can't continue living like this. It's time to stop drinking and get focused on what we want out of life. That's all that's going on... we need to be intentional with our direction." Again, I resonated with this. And it was about time he recognized it too! All this understanding and wisdom, indicated he had been dragging his feet against this truth. But that didn't matter now. He was finally recognizing it, and I began to calm as he continued. "Nicole, what you're feeling has happened to me. I know what you're going through. Just come back over and we'll discuss it. It'll all work out. It's just time to make changes."

A sense of peace entered, and it felt good. His words dissipated the fog, and it felt nice. It made sense... he understood, he knew, and it would all come together now. It was time, and all was fine. All I wanted would come to fruition. Although I felt apprehensive to this new-found peace I welcomed the pretense of it. But hey, peace is peace—right? And with that in mind, I got dressed and headed back to Brad's house.

Chapter 2

My Family

"Mom, I'm going to Brad's," I said as I was leaving. She was watching Chip, my seven-year-old son. He's the one great thing that came out of my broken marriage.

There's a discordant thread of continuity weaving throughout my relationships that has imposed itself so naturally—it feels ingrained. Its presence is a constant companion... a familiar voice to validate the devious ways of men. In fact, my current relationship with Brad was mirroring my parents' relationship a little too closely for my liking. Things needed to change. I knew this, but change was unattainable when I tried to save my marriage. No, wait... now that I think about it, this presence, this discordant thread was already present with my first boyfriend, Clay.

Like most people, my parents were my first example of a relationship. My earliest memories involved going to church as a family, but that stopped when I was around seven. I suppose that became etched in my memory because of the abrupt absence of it. I remember the last day we went to church. The day was much like today—it was a vivid, clear, crisp day. I remember returning from Church and seeing my father trimming the hedges as we slowed to pull into the driveway. He loved caring for his yard. Unknown to me at that time, he, a deacon in the church, had fallen into an affair that would hence forth keep us from church. My mother went to the church about the affair hoping that would help. But instead of his stopping the affair he stopped going to church. I can only assume that he turned away from God and Church because they made him feel bad about the affair. The affair lasted approximately eight years. And to muddy the water even further, when the affair ended, she remained his friend. That's weird I know, and it played a huge part in shaping the fragile areas of my life. As the affair lingered, my parents struggled at best. The drinking started, which opened the door to other struggles, and my mother's life and marriage entered into survival mode.

When she married Dad, she moved thousands of miles away from her friends and family. He was in the Air Force in the first years of their marriage, and she was alone with a toddler and twin babies (I'm one of the twins). I'm one of four children, and Mama worked full time. My brothers and I were fed, clothed, and we had a roof over our heads, therefore job done—right? Well... half done—maybe. To us children, the fights we witnessed became our teacher, too. On Dad's good days, he was a stern dad or a happy drinker. On the bad days, he'd drink and pick fights with Mom, and sometimes he was violent. Most of the time, he was mentally abusive and just mean-spirited. My siblings and I were so familiar with those traits that when he came home we'd retreat to our rooms. "Stay clear of Dad"—that was our motto.

Mom waited on Dad hand and foot, so the fights he picked made no sense at all. Later, I understood that the drinking, as well as picking the fights were guilt motivated. He felt guilty about the affair, so he drank. When he drank, he'd look for reasons to excuse his affair. And I suppose when drinking reasons are validated which causes a need for continuous drinking. It's a vicious cycle. This ritual became a rinse-and-repeat lifestyle that became our normal. I thought other families lived the same way with the same struggles, but what was typical to us, I eventually learned was not typical to other families. But as a child, I didn't know this. For instance, the normality of coming home from school to find the electricity turned off, or the water, or the phone... whichever bill Dad forgot to pay that month—was not normal to other families. Rest assured, once he became aware of it, he'd rectify it by the end of the day, or the next business day—which sometimes fell after the weekend. This lifestyle was normal to us. I now understand that the affair captured his attention and created chaos in our home.

My friend, who lived behind us, also went to our church. Her family eventually pulled away from us. Again, as an adult I understand why. As a child, I couldn't figure out why distance was building in our friendship. Much later, my mother told me how my friend's mom knew about Dad. And since it was getting worse and not better, it made sense that they pulled away. Yet Mom felt alone, and she was alone. My hat has always been off to her for the job she did. I applaud her valor!

A couple of fights stand out to me. One happened when Dad had been working in the yard all day. He started drinking that afternoon, and Mama went to the store. While she was gone, he finished his yard work and sat on the porch to rest and take in his handiwork. He fell asleep there. When Mama got home, she had a headache, which often turned into migraines for her, so she went to lie down. I was lying on the couch watching TV and Dad came inside and asked (with a glare), "Where's your Mom?" I answered, "She had a headache and went to lie down." He went across the room to the kitchen and got a drink of water. He then opened a cabinet and began taking plates out one at a time and throwing them across the room. So many plates were breaking. The funny thing is that I just lay there—ignoring that it was even happening. What? How weird is that? I lay there with my eyes fixed on the TV, ignoring the crashing plates. I suppose it was a coping mechanism. As an adult, I wonder what he thought about this child totally ignoring his behavior. I don't know which is stranger, his behavior or mine? I guess I learned survival-mode from my mother.

When he was finished throwing plates, he left the kitchen and went to their bedroom. The arguing began. He was mad because she didn't wake him and the mosquitos had feasted on him. He was irrational and hit her a few times and also broke a window. And I retreated to my room.

Another fight that stands out to me is when I woke to her pleading for her life as he threatened to pull the trigger saying, "You don't think I'll shoot you?" I lay there in terror, pleading to God for her life and for them to stop fighting.

On another occasion I woke to their fighting, and Mama ran past my room with Daddy chasing her with rifle in hand. He caught her in the kitchen and dragged her back to the bedroom. I guess he went to the bathroom because the next thing I knew, she was gathering me and my brothers, taking us to the car. He came running out the front door just as she was shutting the car door. Mom didn't have time to turn the car around, so she began backing down the street. We lived on a dead-end street, so there was only one way off our street.

Dad got into the other car, and he was driving forward and following us, as we were driving backwards. So there we were, backing down the road with his headlights shining directly onto us as he followed in close proximity. Our street curved onto another street, and when we reached that curve, we backed into a driveway to correct our reversed-driving position to a forward-driving position, but this took too long, and he was soon upon us. He didn't slow down at all. He drove right into our car. Then he backed up and hit us again, then again, and again. It was surreal... like something you'd see in a movie.

He got out of the car and came to Mom's window and told her to drive the car back home, offering threats if she didn't. She had to go back home. She had no choice. And we drove back home with him following us.

While driving back home, she told my twin brother to call the police. When we got to the house, he ran into the house and called the police. He hung up quickly and ran out the back door. He ran off into the neighborhood, and we learned later that he crawled into a neighbor's boat and slept through most of the night, there. Before the sun rose, he came back to the house and slept in the back of the car. My oldest brother slept under the car that night: how terrified he must have been. I eventually went into the house and slept, and the police never came. Turns out that Mama called them and told them not to come because he had fallen asleep. Those were different days then—they took her word for it. Today there's no way they wouldn't have come, especially if a child called.

Before you judge Mama too quickly, she tried to leave several times. On several occasions, we made it halfway to California (to her family), only for

Dad to catch up to us and beg her to come back, promising to change. A couple of times, we actually made it to California, only to return with his promises of change. And there were several occasions when she talked of divorce, and they would go so far as to tell us. Once after gathering us to tell us, he got on his knees and begged her to stay. Again, he promised to change. I remember believing him and hoping that she would, too.

Eventually there was too much water under the bridge, and I began to wish that he was dead. I kept thinking life would be easier if he was gone. Between those intermittent feelings, there were internal questions that continued to emerge. Questions such as, Why was I even born? I didn't ask to be here. What's life about? Life made no sense to me. Everyone does the same thing—day in and day out. We were all in the same lot. Children go to school while parents go to work. Everyone eats and drinks, and all that cycles in and out of our bodies the same way... only to do the same activities all over again. This same lot falls to everyone. We're born, we go to school, we get a job, have families, all the while eating and drinking and recycling that food and drink. Every day, it's rinse and repeat. In fact, if we don't eat and drink—we die. And eventually everyone dies. So, what's it all about? It made no sense to me. Especially when born to a disruptive home. This was my life, and my parents were my example of a marriage, and I didn't ask to be here. So why was I?

When I was growing up, Mama often said, "Nicole, don't get married. Men will only hurt you. They'll cheat on you and lie to you. You can't trust any of them." My dad's example proved the truth of her words. I didn't realize how much this would impact my view of relationships, but it did. How could it not? It came to fruition with my first boyfriend, Clay, and the discordant thread manifested itself.

Chapter 3

The Truth of Mom's Words

To be sure, Clay was a cutie! But I was vain. I hated the shoes he wore. They were ugly enough to kill any attraction I could've had for him. However, once we met, he stayed glued to me. He was literally around me every day. I got so used to him being there that I ended up liking him regardless of his shoes, and we started dating.

He was at my house all the time. We spent all our time together, yet early in our relationship, my lack of trust became evident. Whenever he was late, I wondered where he had been and why he was late. He was a fabulous artist and was also a great drummer in a band. Get the picture? He was a good looking, creative guy in a band. I was always accusing and suspicious of him, and we often argued over my lack of trust.

After more than two years of dating, he began telling me about an office party that was still a few weeks away. He thought it'd be a good trust barometer for me if he went to the party alone. It made no sense to me, and it angered me and made me suspicious. But then again, I was always suspicious. We fought over this party for three weeks. The night before the party, he was still pushing to go alone. I didn't understand it and was highly suspicious. We got into a huge fight.

The next morning, I woke to find him sleeping in his car outside my house. I invited him inside, and we continued discussing the importance of this test for my trust issues. Why was he picking this party to prove my trust? I didn't understand, and I didn't trust it... at all. And because I didn't trust this testing process or him, I saw the need to begin trusting, so I agreed to embrace the test. I literally made up my mind to trust him. I kid you not. It was like flipping a switch. I knew trust needed to be in place for a good relationship. So to stretch myself and prove to me and him both that I could trust... I'd let him go to the office party without me. I didn't like it. But if our relationship was going to make it, I knew I needed to conquer this trust issue. I knew my trust would endure this test, and we'd be better for it. It was decided, and from deep within me, I was determined.

So he went to the party without me, and I went out to eat dinner with my family, who by now was on the backside of the horrible fights now that the affair had ended. On the way home, they asked me where Clay was. I said, "He's probably kissing some girl right now," but I was quick to inwardly check that lack of trust attitude and said, "No, he's at an office party." To this day, I know the exact place we were driving when I spoke those words. I was so intentional with my thoughts and was hanging my hat on this trust factor. I knew I would conquer it, and we'd be better for it—because I could now trust.

We got home, and my older brother was leaving to go to a friend's apartment and asked if I wanted to go with him. I said, "No, I'm just going to stay home tonight." He went on without me, and I was cleaning my room when Mom yelled for me to come to the phone. My brother had called me.

"Hello... Nicole..." he said, "...I came to Mason's, and there's a party at his club house, and as I drove past, I saw Clay kissing some girl." My heart sank. I could not believe what was happening. My mind raced over the past fights about this party. The point of contention was always my lack of trust. On the heels of all those "party-fights," I drove a trust-stake right into the foundation of our relationship and my heart. It would prove I could in fact trust him and would lay a better foundation for our future relationship. I had made up my mind to trust. AND WHAT HAPPENED?!?!?!? Mama's words rang true! You can't trust men!!! You really can't! Mama was right! I couldn't believe this was happening. I couldn't believe that I decided to

14

trust, and less than twenty-four hours later, Mama's words were proven true. To say the least, I was devastated.

I went directly to my room and grabbed all Clay's artwork—all the beautiful oil paintings he had given me. One was of Christ, with his face depicted from the Shroud of Turin. He was wearing the crown of thorns and the robe they draped over him after beating him. Christ was standing in a doorway with daylight illuminating from behind him. His head was down, but he was glancing up as if looking at Pontius Pilot. Clay had also inscribed a beautiful poem his father wrote called "I Am" over it. His father was a pastor, and the poem was beautiful. I actually asked Clay for it several times. Then, when I was in the hospital with pneumonia, I woke up to see it leaning against the wall in my hospital room. I felt so loved. He gave me many sketches along with other poems throughout our relationship. He was very creative and romantic. I gathered everything he gave me and put them in the car.

It was raining as I sped off to that party. On the way, I looked at the painting of Christ and said, "I'm sorry for what I'm about to do." When I got there, I parked right outside the clubhouse. I went inside and saw him sitting with her against a wall. I walked over and grabbed his hand. He didn't resist. He got up immediately and followed me to my car. He stood there in the rain as I turned and bent into my car to retrieve those items and bent, tore, and threw them onto the soaked pavement. The glass in the framed drawings broke when hitting the ground. All the while, I told him what I thought of him and his art. My voice was coming out of the depths of my being. I was in agonizing grief.

When I finished, I stormed off, and he followed. He stopped me and tried to stop me from breaking up with him. But how could he? The entire time, not one tear left my eyes... only this agonizing, heart-wrenching, angered grief emanating from me as I yelled and groaned in disbelief. I turned away from him and went to find my brother, and he drove me home.

The following morning, as soon as my eyes opened, tears gushed forth. I lay there in silence as streams of incessant tears poured from me as I curled into the fetal position. I was devastated on two accounts: One for the betrayal and the other because I realized the truth of my mother's words that you can never trust a man... never. As I mulled things over, I examined how I felt. I hurt so badly. How did this happen? It's really over? I would never see him again... really?

A couple of hours passed, and he called. He begged me to give him another chance. As I listened to him, I realized how desperately I'd miss him. I decided to take him back so I wouldn't hurt so much, and then I'd work on getting over him while I was still with him. Talk about manipulation. At his request, we went to see a movie that afternoon. I remember feeling so dead and numb inside, but at the same time thinking, at least I'm with him. And I recognized this as the first step in my journey to get over him.

I began taking more time between our visits and calls. I would choose going out with my friends instead of seeing him. And I didn't care what he did without me. It simply didn't matter to me. I had a plan. When push came to shove, he knew something was wrong. He began asking that we spend more time together and questioning my behavior. I never questioned him or his motives about anything. He should have been happy... right? From his perspective, he should've thought I trusted him. Right? I did remain true to him and I assured him of this. But the bitter unspoken truth was... that while I was not dating around, I was in fact getting over him.

One night, he started interrogating me to find out why I seemed so indifferent. I assured him I was not cheating on him, but I argued that I didn't need to spend all my time with him. And that he could hang with his friends all he wanted to. He felt we should break up, and I let it happen. He tried to retract it, but it was too late. The words were spoken, and I was over him. It was over, and I was good with that. He, on the other hand, was devastated. In retrospect, I can't blame him. On my part... it was all so calculated. I wanted to get over him while I was still with him, and that's exactly what I did.

My next relationship took me into my marriage with Kurt. All the warning signs were there, and I should have paid attention and run. But he seemed like such a good-ole-boy, and because of that, I thought I'd hit the jackpot! So I thought. Years later, my marriage did end, and I found myself living back home with my parents.

Flash forward a year or so, and I met Brad, and we started dating. Then one day, Clay spontaneously showed up at my parent's house. We all visited for a while, and then Clay and I walked outside. He took my arm to get my attention. I turned to look at him, and he said, "Nicole, I want to tell you again how sorry I am for all I did wrong in our relationship and how I hurt you."

"Oh Clay," I responded, "...don't even think about it again. There's no need to apologize. We were both young and dumb."

He laughed in agreement. Then he said, "Nicole, I still love you. In fact, I've never stopped."

I looked away, then at him and said, "Clay, I've forgiven you for everything. Thank you for stopping by to tell me you're sorry, but there was no need for that. Please know you are forgiven, and please know that we will always be friends." He knew what I meant. I could tell he did. I was honored that he came by to tell me his thoughts and feelings. But I couldn't help how things had changed. His actions changed things. Later as I drove to Brad's, I contemplated how things could have been different had I indeed been able to trust Clay that fateful night of the office party.

Chapter 4

Wrong Benchmark

My choice to get over Clay while still dating him seemed so logical at the time and it worked. The abrupt pain of his betrayal of my trust was so hard to bear, and to think that I'd never see him again on top of that... this compounded my grief. One small decision to get over him while with him altered life for me. His choice to betray my trust altered life for him. Dad's choice to have the affair altered life for our entire family. Choices affect us in so many ways, yet it's funny how we spend so little time contemplating them and their cause and effects.

Although my early years definitely influenced my life, as a teenager I seemed to navigate by comparing my life to those around me. In high school you encounter so many people, and the stories there are wide and varied. I knew so many girls with no boundaries. They predetermined to have sex with whomever they chose to, and they did. I determined that I would wait for love. They also fancied trying various drugs and drinking at parties, and they did.

I finally decided it was time to see what this drinking was all about and planned to spend the night with a friend while her parents were out of town. We were finally going to dip our toes into the pool of teenage drinking to see what it was all about. We were young and stupid, but when comparing ourselves to others, we were still good girls. All she had in her house for us to drink was a half-bottle of vodka and one 16-ounce cola. That's right, it was vodka and cola. I know it sounds nasty, and it was! And the ratio in each glass was about 1/4 cola and 3/4 vodka, which made it worse. It was AWFUL, but we were determined to get drunk to see what it was like.

Well, we achieved our goal. At first, we were silly and laughing at everything. But that all flew south as things began to fly north—with the room spinning and the vomiting, all through the night. The next morning when I felt good enough to leave, I went home.

That evening, I began getting ready to go to a teenage dance place that my brothers and I frequented. My mother happened to be going somewhere too and was in the bathroom putting her makeup on at the same time. I was drinking a lot of water and came back from refilling my glass when my mother asked, "Have you been drinking?"

What? How did she know? I looked at her in shock and asked, "How did you know?"

She said, "You're drinking so much water, which happens after a night of heavy drinking." Who knew that was a sign of a drinking a lot? Obviously, she knew... and now so did I. And now she knew the truth. However, I did make up my mind to never drink again and I informed her of this. Drinking was a stupid endeavor of which I wanted no part.

That incident proved to be a good barrier throughout my teenage years. Though my friends drank at parties, I didn't. When they used drugs, I abstained. While they chose to have sex, I waited for love. So you see, by comparison I was a good girl. The problem was that my benchmark was wrong. I knew nothing of this at that age... we were simply following each other around. It was going to take years for me to understand this benchmark and comparison system I had in place. But for the teenage years with absentee parents, it was the only benchmark I had to navigate my life and relationships.

So I went dancing regularly with my brothers, and while everyone else drank alcohol and got drunk, I drank sodas and danced. This was my weekend routine until the teenage dance place closed. My brothers found other things to do while my friends and I went to parties or movies. Then

I learned that my oldest brother had been going to a full-fledged dance bar. Of course, we were too young to go there, but he managed to get in and taught the rest of us the ropes. The first time I went with my brothers, they introduced me to their friends. One guy was an extremely tall guy named Bill. They introduced him to me, saying, "This is our sister Nicole, and you're the only guy we want to marry her." I couldn't believe they said that! But I knew it meant they liked him—a lot.

He asked me to dance, and out on the dance floor we went. I started dancing and looked at him to see him not dancing but standing there with a puzzled look while staring at me. I gave him a questioning look that said, "What?" He said, "What are you doing?" This didn't help answer my question at all. I said, "Dancing! What else?" To which he replied while laughing, "Oh that's not dancing!"

Okay, so maybe I wasn't the best dancer, but I was keeping rhythm. I liked to dance and I liked dance music. I know I'm capable of keeping a beat. I feel it all the time. But perhaps my one visit to ballet class altered my perception of dancing. I have no idea... I'm grasping at straws here. What I thought was dancing was alternately moving my legs to tap my toes on an imaginary line in front of me. All while holding my arms up to almost shoulder height while swaying them to the music. It sure seemed like dancing to me. I just stopped and shrugged saying, "What's wrong with it?" He said, "Do this." And he began dancing. I watched him, and it did look really cool. He was standing in the same spot. His feet weren't doing anything fancy like mine. He looked calm, sophisticated, attractive, and sure of himself, much like Will Smith in the movie Hitch. To be sure, I did not look like that, but I didn't think I was far from it.

I tried to mimic him. It was like patting your head and rubbing your stomach at the same time. It wasn't happening. He demonstrated again and I tried again, to no avail. He demonstrated more slowly. I still couldn't get it. His shoulders were alternately moving up and down while his hips were moving in the opposite direction of his shoulders. It looked incredibly cool but I couldn't do it AT ALL. I finally pulled him off the dance floor and found a discrete place for him to continue instructing me.

Finally he told me to place my hands on my thighs and move my shoulders. Then add my hips to the equation. And it was like some magic pill! It at least helped me feel the rhythm of it. I began to slowly put it to the music while not lifting my hands off my legs. If I removed my hands from my thighs it all went awry. It was like losing your balancing pole on the high wire. Eventually we made our way back to the dance floor, and I was able to move to the pace of the music. And by the end of the night I could let my hands stray from my legs every now and then. It only took a couple of nights dancing with Bill for me to get the hang of this new move... and with this I earned his approval to my future dancing. Thanks to him I was now a better dancer who actually knew how to dance.

Bill was a great teacher, and I was a great student. I loved dancing with Bill, and he did prove to be a great guy, but he just wasn't my type. I was sorry to disappoint my brothers, but the guy I married would have to be my type.

We continued going to the dance bar until someone informed the manager of our true ages. However, I think he really knew we weren't old enough, but he flirted with me all the time and didn't give it a second thought. In fact, he found a way around the problem for me. He convinced me to try my hand at bartending. Who knew I was old enough to work there, just not to frequent there as a patron? He said, "Why not work and get paid where all your friends come hang out? I can promise that you'll make more money than you do at your retail job."

"But..." I said, "I don't know how to bartend." He continued, "No worries, I'll train you. What do you say?" It was so tempting, since the upscale clothing chain I worked for was closing. The next retail job I was looking into had a policy stating you had to be twenty-one to be in management—and I was only eighteen. I was an assistant manager at my current job, and since I had to wait to grow into management there, I decided to give bartending a try. And he was right. It was a blast, and I made a lot of money!

It's so bizarre how I was literally surrounded with co-workers and customers who loved doing the very thing I thought so stupid... drinking. I was the only bartender there who didn't drink or do drugs.

Chapter 5

My Marriage

It was through bartending that I met my husband Kurt. After work, we often went out to eat. The only places open at that hour were breakfast restaurants. Kurt was the manager of one such place. He was finishing school and working nights there. He was cute and had a sweet southern-gentleman disposition. I thought he was a true good-ole-boy. He started hanging out with us regularly. After eating, we'd go to someone's apartment and play cards until the sun rose.

This kind of lifestyle goes with working nights. The thing that should have made me run the other direction was the fact that Kurt was married. On those late nights that turned into mornings, we became friends. I thought it so strange, though, how he could stay out all night long on a regular basis. I began to imagine his wife as being a horrible person. His staying out all night and his reason for doing so didn't matter to me because we were just friends. It was his business if he stayed out all night... I wasn't his wife, so why should it matter to me? But a man and a woman can't hang out all hours of the night without things eventually changing. And eventually, our friendship made a turn. I was soon coming up with excuses for his horrible marriage. Soon they divorced, and soon after that... we were married.

I became pregnant right away, and when my son Chip was born, a love exploded from my heart that enveloped me. I couldn't believe it. I never imagined the capacity for that kind of love. We all know we're going to love our children. We all hear the stories about that love being instantaneous, but I had no idea the amount of love that would emanate from me for him.

In fact, as a young teenager, I declared I didn't want kids. You see, I had a dream of being a successful buyer for a high-end clothing store in New York. I'd have a fancy New York apartment with white furniture and white carpet, a white jeep, and a beautiful white Afghan Hound dog. Children would get in the way of that dream. A child and that life don't go together. Thankfully, that dream didn't come to fruition, because I had no idea about love like this! The trajectory of my heart had changed, and it changed in just a moment of time.

After becoming a mama, I no longer wanted to work as a bartender. I no longer wanted to work, period. I wanted to be a stay-at-home mom and care for my child, but that wasn't possible. Our household budget needed my income. I mentioned the possibility of my going to cosmetology school to Kurt, but he absolutely forbade it. His reasoning? He didn't want me touching other men—in any capacity. At the time it made no sense to me. He would rather me serve men drinks than cut their hair because he didn't want me touching them? However, hindsight's 20/20, and on the backside of my marriage, I can see it had everything to do with his cheating lifestyle. He didn't trust me in that type of job because he was untrustworthy. Soon enough, I would discover his cheating habits and would understand why he thought like that. He was seeing through his own warped lenses.

The reason I wanted to go to cosmetology school was to eventually own my own business and be in control of my own hours. But I honored how he felt and didn't pursue it, although I would get out of bartending— eventually. For the first year of Chip's life though, we managed for me to stay home with him.

Once he began walking, we decided I would work an office job and put Chip in a day care that was close to my parent's house. A few weeks before this transition, I purchased a huge, stuffed bear for him. He would take this to day care and I hoped it would remind him of home. A few weeks later, we both reported to our new life—he at his day care to meet new friends,

and me at my office job. I dropped him and bear off on my way to work...
and I cried the entire way to work.

At lunch, I decided to go visit him. I walked in, and the other children
were on the playground playing. Chip was sitting in the doorway beside his
bear. He was there all alone watching the other kids play. He was silhouetted
by the light from outside. I knelt behind him and whispered his name,
"Chip." He turned to me and in his fourteen-month-old little way, began
shaking and crying as he reached for me with a thankful, desperate look on
his face. I withdrew him immediately and quit my office job. I didn't even
go back after lunch; I just called them and told them I wouldn't be back.

A month or so later, I went back to work at the five-star hotel where
Kurt worked. My mother was an angel and continued to watch Chip. Sadly,
over the next two years, Kurt demonstrated the same habits he had in
his first marriage. He stayed out all night long, and on his nights off from
work, he chose to go out with friends rather than staying home with us,
and he drank a lot. I was still not drinking. Remember my lesson? It was
still holding true for me. I cried and begged him to change and to make us
a priority, but he would not.

Many fights and tears later when nothing had changed, I thought,
perhaps we should incorporate Church into our life. Perhaps that will help.

Chapter 6

Saving My Marriage

Thinking about going to Church to make things right was not a strange thing to me. You see, I thought I was a Christian since childhood because of an experience I had when we were still going to church. I was sitting in church, and the preacher said that without Christ as Lord and Savior, one cannot enter heaven. Well... I didn't want to go to hell, so I thought it was a good idea to sign up with Christ. I went down front to get my get out of hell free card, and I got Jesus!

The preacher came over the following week to discuss the Bible. He recommended that I read it but suggested that I not read the book of Revelation. Not at first anyway. I thought it was extremely odd that a preacher would tell me not to read a particular book of the Bible. And of course, whenever I decided to start reading the Bible, I always began with the book of Revelation. I can be stubborn.

Many things happened in the years that unfolded between that little girl and the third year of my marriage. I met a few Christians during those years, from my mother's side of the family, and their behavior was always foreign to me. They talked about their relationship with God and how they interacted with him daily. I never had a clue about the things they discussed. Why was there such a difference? I couldn't tell you, because I didn't understand it.

Flash forward several years, and there I was in a struggling marriage with a son. This seemed as good a time as any to read the Bible. One night, Kurt was out with friends, and I put Chip to bed and decided to begin reading the Bible, and of course I turned right to the book of Revelation to begin that journey.

As I read, the Scriptures began speaking to my heart. I thought this was a sign to get my life on track and save my marriage. I wanted to visit churches, but Kurt didn't care anything about going with me. My reading the Bible didn't last long, but I did visit a couple of churches. Eventually, a girl I worked with said she'd visit some churches with me. One Sunday, she came over to go to church with me. Kurt stood there as we scrambled to get out the door (not helping at all) and said, "Wouldn't it be great if Nicole became a Christian?" What? I couldn't believe he said that. At least I was trying!

I spent a lot of the last two years of my marriage crying and begging him to change. I begged him to come home after work instead of going out with his friends. He wouldn't, and he didn't. He went out with them nightly. One night while I was at work, he came in to see the show with his friends. I introduced Kurt to my boss and took Kurt and his friends to their table. My boss later came up to me, and pointing at Kurt she said, "He's your husband?"

I said, "Yes. Why?"

She said, "Nicole, I was at a party two weeks ago, and he slept with Susan." Susan was a bartender at another restaurant in the hotel.

I shrugged my shoulders and said, "That doesn't surprise me," and walked away. I tried to hide how embarrassed, hurt, and angry I really was.

I went to the back to fill drink orders, and another bartender held a Fuzzy Navel out to me. It's a fruity drink that's served up chilled and without ice. He said, "Here Nicole," while looking around to see if anyone was coming, and said, "I made the wrong drink for the customer. Drink it." I didn't care, I knew what he was doing. He was trying to make me feel better. So I drank it quickly and thought, that didn't taste bad at all! In fact, it tasted worlds away from vodka and cola... It was pretty tasty. Then as the night went on, lie held out another one and another. By the third one, I noticed I didn't really care about too many things, much less my cheating husband. And right here is where I began to realize why people drink. It makes you not care—for the moment.

Eventually, I realized that I didn't want Kurt to be a role model for Chip, and I asked him to leave. A co-worker moved in with me and life continued. Kurt eventually moved out of state and pursued the divorce.

I went out from time to time with my friends, and I began to drink with them. It was something I thought I'd never do. It was in moderation and not that frequent until... Brad came into my life.

Chapter 7

Brad

After my divorce, I eventually moved back home with my parents. I needed to re-evaluate and get prepared to raise my son—by myself. I decided to go to cosmetology school, and my mother quit working to watch Chip for me.

This season catapulted the journey of making peace with my father. He had already done an about-face when he became a grandfather. To my shock, he was a wonderful grandfather. I never anticipated it... not in a million years. And there I was, back at home, and because he was an involved grandfather, it brought up discussions of my childhood experiences.

One day while my father was at work, we got into a conversation on the phone. I reminded him of what we witnessed as children and told him how there were times I wished he were dead. He cried and asked me to forgive him, and I did, but it was a little harder for Mom. She still loved him, but she was no longer in love with him. Harsh living with him had taken its toll, but our family was together. Mom stayed, and our family was still intact. I wasn't sure how to navigate this healing road, but we were on it and time would tell all.

I was on the road to getting my life on track. I had a dream of doing hair and makeup for movies, and cosmetology school was the first step. I went back to work at that bar I first worked at as a bartender. This was only part time, since school was full time, forty hours per week. I had to work to have a little money to pay bills, and that's where I met Brad. He would come in, and we'd talk, and we eventually started dating.

By comparison (my benchmark), my relationship with Brad was the best one up to this point in my life. However, with time, it also proved to be the worst. The best is what kept me with him. He took me places I'd never been and treated me like a queen. At other times, he was manipulative and controlling. And all the while... we drank. If we went out to eat, we drank. If we went out on the boat, we drank. If we went on vacations, we drank. If we just stayed in for the night, we drank. I began to wonder if we would drink every day for the rest of our lives.

He proposed several times, and I said "yes" several times, and he broke up with me several times. During our breakups, he always dated other women. He would eventually call me, and we'd get back together. Over time, he manipulated me to the point where I believed that he was the best man I could ever get by causing me to believe that no man would marry someone with a child. And I felt lucky to be wanted by him. So, whenever he'd break up with me, I was devastated—believing that my chances to ever be married again were gone.

A few weeks would go by with each breakup, and just when I'd think that this time it was for good, he'd call, and we'd get back together. This cycle continued for three years, but I was committed because I didn't want another failed relationship. I was determined that this relationship would make it. I truly believed that after we got married, things would calm down, and we'd start going to church and then do family life together. I thought marriage and church would fix it, but our engagements never made it to the wedding day.

Once, it looked as if we might make it to the wedding day, and then I couldn't handle it. I started getting cold feet. For instance, one morning when he was in the shower, he blew his nose, and I thought, can you put up with that—every day for the rest of your life? I could sense I was looking for reasons to call it off. That was short-lived because he beat me to it. He called it off again, and just when I was convinced it was over... he called to get back together, and we did.

He knew I wanted us to start going to church, and he assured me that we would—when we got married. Again, as in my marriage, I eventually started visiting churches by myself, and one day he said to me, "What's going to happen to us if you become a Christian?" I thought, that's a great question. I simply shrugged and concealed the fact that I wondered the same thing.

Chapter 8

Church

It's weird how things happen to connect all the dots in life. Things that happen and our responses to them become threads that weave the substances of our life together.

One such time happened in my teenage years when I was out with my friends. Life seemed fine enough: school was fine, home was fine and friendships were fine. It was fall—October to be exact. Haunted houses were up and active all over the city. I wasn't a fan of haunted houses, but we happened upon one that was hosted by a church. We all thought it strange enough to warrant a visit.

First we entered this dilapidated house with cobwebs everywhere. We heard creaking sounds as we walked. Seated around the dining table were "dead" people with cobwebs draped over them. There were mice here and there. This was not my cup of tea, but as long as no masked guy with a chainsaw was jumping out at me, I was fine. It was better than most haunted houses I had visited. I can't remember the rest of our house tour... probably because of what happened when we were guided out the back door and into the huge moonlit landscape.

Across a wide-open field sat a tent-pavilion and this was our final destination. As we got closer, we could see an open grave with a pile of dirt next to it, with a coffin on a stand beside the open grave. There were chairs for us to have a seat at this graveside service. We took our seats. A man walked up to begin the funeral service. He began talking about the five points of life and death. I can't remember the points he made, but at that time, they resonated with me. I was the only one out of my friends who was crying and who stayed behind to talk with the man. We talked, and he prayed with me. I went home and told Mom all about it and told her I wanted to visit the church.

The next week I received a handwritten letter from the pastor, who turned out to be the man at the graveside. I was touched that he took the time to write. I planned on visiting the church, but I never got around to it. A few years later, I learned they built a school, and I declared that if I ever had kids, they would go to that school.

It's strange how I never visited that church, even during the previous church-visiting seasons. Over the past year, I had thought about visiting it several times, but something always happened to keep me away or directed me elsewhere. The day finally did come when I visited it. But getting there was no easy task. I planned on going one Sunday, but I woke up late. Of course I did. Like most good intentions go, going to church that Sunday morning flew south. Just like all the past Sundays.

There was something different, though, about this Sunday morning. I was tired of the same old routine that kept me from church. The same old saying that I'd go but never making it. Why couldn't I make it to church? Why was this such a hard thing to do? As I was thinking about this, it occurred to me to shake things up a bit. Why couldn't I go that Sunday evening instead? Churches have a Sunday evening services too. Then I wondered why that thought had never occurred to me before. That didn't matter—it occurred to me now, and it was decided. Chip and I would go to Sunday evening service. And with that decision made, I went about my day.

My father was in an exceptionally good mood that day. It was unusually cold for that time of year: it felt cold enough to snow, but it rarely snows in these parts. He and Mom were doing some deep cleaning, and I decided to join in the efforts and deep clean my room, too. Then Kati, a friend from work, called. "Hey Kati, what's up?"

"Hey Nicole, want to go ice skating?" she asked.

"What? Ice skating? I'd love to!" was my response.

She continued, "A few of us are meeting there."

I couldn't believe what I was hearing. There was a new ice-skating rink in town, and I had been wanting to try it. Ice skating is my favorite part of the Olympics, and I couldn't wait to get to that rink and try my hand at it. As a girl I used to go roller skating and loved that. How much more fun would it be to glide on ice? I said, "Count me in, what time are we meeting?"

"Oh good! Let's meet at 5:45 sound good?" she responded.

"Oh, I thought you were talking about this afternoon. I can't go tonight."

"Why not?" she asked.

I knew I was about to sound like a weirdo. She won't understand. Then, surprising to me, my internal wrestling began. Why can't you go to church another day? Next week? It's no big deal. And why do you even want to go on a Sunday night? Doesn't real church take place in the mornings? These were questions I would expect to hear from Kati, not from myself. After all, I had never mentioned church or God to her. I swallowed and said, "I promised myself I would go to church this morning and didn't make it. In frustration with myself, I committed to go tonight. I've tried to visit this church for years, and I've never made it. If I don't go today, I may never make it. There's always something standing in the way. So I'm going tonight. How about we go skating this afternoon?" I was hoping to make both happen.

"Everyone else is going tonight. After that, we're going out to Shannigans. Just make up your mind to go next week and come with us tonight."

This was such a hard decision. I so wanted to go with them. I sat there for an awkward moment, you know, those that seem way longer than they really are. I finally said, "I'll have to go next time. I'm going to church tonight. If you guys want to go this afternoon I can go, otherwise, I can't go." I was so sad to say no. I really wanted to go skating, but I knew there was always something to keep me from going to this church. And it was bizarre for her to call me on a Sunday and ask me to go do something I wanted to do for a while. It was hard to say no, but I did.

She said, "Okay, well we're going tonight. If you change your mind, let me know."

Wow, that didn't go as awkwardly as I thought it would. There was no balking, no trying to talk me out of it—she accepted it. She threw the temptation out there for me to change my mind, but she accepted my decision. I took a deep breath and said, "Sure... maybe we can go next week?" We exchanged a few more casual comments and got off the phone, and I got back to my deep cleaning on this wintry day.

Later that afternoon, my dad stuck his head in my room and happily announced that he was going to grill steaks. He enjoyed grilling, and even though it felt like winter, he would not be detoured from doing one of his favorite things. Only rain could keep him from grilling. I smiled and said, "Oh that sounds great!" He smiled back and walked down the hall. He was drinking, and this exaggerated his good mood. I knew when he found out I was going to church it would ruin his mood... especially when hearing that I was taking Chip with me. Chip was his buddy. He loved spending time with him. I dreaded his finding out. I kept cleaning. Eventually I told Mom about my plans. I think I hoped I could sneak out, and she could deliver the bad news to him. It didn't work out that way.

He was in the kitchen preparing the steaks. I had to walk through there to get my purse. I grabbed it and said, "Come on Chip," while walking to the front room.

"Where are y'all going?" Dad asked.

I said, "To church," as if this were a normal happenstance for me.

He immediately was taken aback. "What? Why? I told you I was cooking out."

As he gestured to the steaks I said, "I know, and we're looking forward to eating when we get home."

This did not ease his frustration. "Why are you going on a Sunday night? Why not go next week on Sunday morning?"

This made sense to me too. Normal people who want to visit a church typically do so on a Sunday morning. I knew this. And I didn't know why I had such strong resolve to go this particular Sunday night, but I did. I said, "You know how many Sunday mornings I've been trying to get to church?

Something always comes up. I planned on going this morning, but I woke up late. When I woke up late, I made up my mind to go tonight. So, that's why we're going." I acted as if this was sufficient reason for him, and I turned and said, "Come on Chip." I grabbed my keys.

Then he said, "Why not leave Chip here and let him eat steak with us?"

That sounded reasonable too, but I wanted him to go with me. My mind was made up, and nothing was going to alter it. I said, "No, he's going with me. We'll eat when we get back." He looked very frustrated but what was he going to say? After all, I was the daughter who would from time to time plead with him to take us to church. He made empty promises, but we never went. And now here I stood declaring I would take my son to church. What could he say? Nothing. I felt sorry for the situation, but we walked out the front door to go to church. Victory!

I need to preface what happened next with what my financial situation was like. I was still living with my parents. I was trying to establish my career in cosmetology. I had a car but no insurance; I couldn't afford it. As I walked to my car on that wintry night, it began snowing. I stopped in my tracks. I felt defeated. Normally I would've been excited to see snow, since we rarely get it around here. Suffice it to say that I didn't know how to drive in it—for the lack of it. I stood there. I knew I had no business going anywhere with it snowing. While we were in church, it could pile up outside, making it a treacherous trip home. I said to Chip, "Come on Chip, looks like we're not going after all." He didn't have a clue to the turmoil going on inside me... in fact, he was excited at the snow. We turned around and went back inside. I threw my purse on the table and looked at my parents who looked bewildered at my reappearance. I now exasperated said, "We're not going. It's snowing!" My father smiled, looked excited, and hugged Chip. I sat there. I couldn't believe the obstacles that continued to arise to keep me from church. And then something welled up in me. Something is working against my going to church. I must go. I grabbed my purse and said, "Come on Chip. God will get us home safely. We will trust him. Let's go." And with that and to the shock of my parents, we left.

We were late to church, but we made it. I slipped in the back and found a seat. As we were sitting there listening to the teaching, another girl slipped in and sat beside me. She was later than I was! We smiled as we acknowledged one another. After the service, as I was gathering our things, she introduced herself to me. She extended her hand, "Hey I'm Carol."

"Hey Carol, I'm Nicole, and this is Chip."

She said, "Have you visited before?"

"No," I said, "this is the first time."

Then she did the strangest thing, something never done at any other church I had ever visited. She took out a pen and said, "Well, let me give you my number. If you have any questions, just give me a call and let me know when you visit again, and I'll meet you here."

I smiled. "That sounds good. Thank you." And there it was, the reason I was so committed to getting to church that night and the reason so many things were working against it. Even my tardiness worked to align things for our meeting. I was now connected to someone in the church, and in fact I committed right there to meet her the following Sunday.

I met Carol the following Sunday, and she walked us to a classroom for Chip and his age group, and then we went to a class that she went to. The lady was teaching out of the book of Ruth. I didn't fully understand everything that was going on, but I realized God was moving. I sat in fear and trembling. I knew I had decisions to make. Decisions I didn't want to make. I recognized the truth and veracity of God's word. I sat there as tears began welling. After class I had some questions for the teacher. Carol went on to the church service and left us to talk. We discussed her teaching and what God's word means to us. What God was trying to teach them in the Bible days and us about himself, his love for us, and his provision of Christ. I cried even more. She then asked me, "Nicole, do you want to receive Christ as your Lord and Savior?"

I said, "I do, but I can't." I couldn't believe what I said. I looked at her and said, "I can't because I don't think he would want me to be with the guy I'm with, and I'm not willing to let him go." I couldn't believe I said that. But I knew our past and his betrayals. I knew his partying lifestyle. I knew he was concerned about my becoming a Christian. I knew the two didn't go together. I couldn't say yes to God. When we walked out of the classroom, the church service was over. I couldn't believe that we talked through the entire church service. Carol met me with Chip. She went and got him for me. When we got in the car, I said to God, "God, I know what I just did. I know I said no to you. Please don't let me die without figuring this out." On the drive home, I played the radio for Chip as I sat in silence.

Chapter 9

Promises

I said no to God two weeks ago, and now here I am driving back to Brad's house. In retrospect, I now realize that the urgency I felt last night to leave, and the returning urgency this morning, was not the first time I felt that nudging presence. I remember once I was on my way to Brad's from work. He asked me to stop and pick up some beer. I remember glancing at the beer in the car and thinking, do we have to drink every day? And now that I think about it, I had a small nudging earlier last night. It came in the form of a question. Brad and I were leaving one bar to go to another one across town. We were crossing the street to go to the car and the nudging question came to me, asking, "How long are you going to keep doing the very thing you don't want to be doing?" I shrugged it off. I realized I didn't want to continue this drinking lifestyle, but I thought it would eventually stop. It had to.

As we sat at the next bar, the music was playing. It was late. Only people who usually stay till closing were there, and most of them had too much to drink. I didn't want to be there. This has to stop, that's all I could think. As it got later, he started treating me like he never had before. Not mean, but in a demeaning and very sexual way. This made me sad but I hid my emotions. I was so happy when we left and were heading back to his place. We had plans for the next day and had decided that I would stay the night.

We got to his place and went straight to bed. Later that night, I woke up with the urgency to leave.

But now, things are different, things are changing. Because I left the note this morning, everything's out in the open. He seemed to understand my urgency to leave. He knew we needed to make changes. I was so relieved and looked forward to making those changes together. It felt great. I was happy it turned out this way and that we were finally going to get on the right road, together.

I walked into his apartment, and we hugged. "It's good to see you, Nicole." He kissed me and hugged me—good and long. This feels nice, it feels right. He stepped back, and looking at me, he said, "I've known for a while that we needed to make changes. It's time. Your note just pushed it along. We both know we can't keep drinking like we've been doing. It's time for us to stop. We both know it... that's all that's going on with you. We'll stop. It's time." Boy that felt good to hear him say. We went to sit down on the couch and turning to me he asked, "Have you eaten yet?"

That was such a normal question. The funny thing was I hadn't thought about food all day. Only now did I have an appetite. "No I haven't."

"Want to go to Thikados?" he asked. This was one of our favorite restaurants. "Sure," I responded. "That sounds great."

When we got there and went on the wait list and decided to wait in the bar. We sat down, and he said, "Since we're going to make this 'change', why not have drinks with dinner... one last time? We'll stop drinking tomorrow." I hesitated but thought, why not? If we're stopping tomorrow... it'll be fine. I agreed and ordered a drink with him, and they eventually called us to our table. Once there, we ordered our dinner, and he ordered another drink. After dinner, we headed back to his place.

On the way back, he asked, "Want to stop at Joe's for one last drink?" Now Joe's was one of our favorite sports bars. I hesitated. He said, while grabbing my hand, "It's just one last one. We'll stop drinking tomorrow, I promise."

I said, "Sure". We walked inside and took a seat at the bar. He ordered us both beers and citrus shooters. The football game was still on TV, and

Brad looked so happy. He was where he wanted to be. The bartender placed the drinks in front of us. Brad slammed his shooter down and started drinking his beer.

I took the shooter to my lips, and tears began streaming down my cheeks. "What's wrong?" he asked.

I just sat there shaking my head and crying. I said, "I want to leave."

He said, "Sure. Just let me finish these." He slammed down my shooter and quickly drank both beers. We walked to the car in silence, and we drove home that way too. We walked into the house. He asked, "What is wrong with you?" I just sat down on the edge of the bed. All I wanted to do was go home. I just sat there with my head down trying to figure out what was going on with me. He came and sat down beside me.

What happened next was surreal. He started speaking to me, but his voice was so low, methodical, and calculated. It didn't sound like him at all. There was a low, gruff-whisper tone to it. It sounded like pure evil. He said, "Who do you think I am?" I couldn't believe the words or the tone that came from him.

I couldn't bring myself to look at him and I certainly didn't want to show any emotional response. It wasn't Brad, I knew that. There was something dark and sinister about it. Not looking at him, I got up, saying, "I need to go to the bathroom." While I was in there, I gathered myself together. Okay... you know you have to leave. Breathe deeply. I inhaled and exhaled slowly. I looked at myself in the mirror. What the heck? I took more deep breaths. Okay, casually open the door. Don't make eye contact. Simply say you need to go. Grab your purse and get the heck out. With hand on knob, I took one last breath and turned it. I swung the door open as if nothing was wrong and said, "Hey, I gotta' go." Looking toward my purse, I grabbed it and walked out the door.

Inside, I was running, and I literally had to make myself walk. It was an internal battle because everything within wanted me to RUN!!! Once outside, I still made myself walk to the car. Why couldn't I run once I was outside? I don't know. I wanted to appear calm and collected. I didn't want whatever or whoever was speaking through him to know they rattled me.

Once I was in the car, the urgency returned, and I couldn't drive home fast enough. I had the shudders and shakes all the way home... as if I were trying to shake off what had just transpired.

Once home, I went straight to bed. My thoughts were swirling. What in the world is happening? I'm trembling like a leaf! I had no peace. I lay there with silence all around me. "God help me. I need you to help me. I need peace. Please God, please. Help me? Oh God, please." I continued crying out to him. What is going on with me? What in the world? I'm a mom; I have got to pull it together. "Please God, give me peace. I'll never get sleep unless you help me. Please help me? Please?" I cried and cried. "Please, God. Help me." As I lay there calling out to him, all of a sudden my entire body snapped like when you pop a knuckle. And there was peace. I wasn't trembling anymore. What in the world? I started to question it but then remembered my prayer and the fact that I had peace. I would not question it. I'd go to sleep in peace... and I did.

Chapter 10

That's a Good Idea

The next morning, my eyes opened as if I were summoned awake. I felt rested, and I could tell it was morning. My thoughts began rolling... Hmmm, the sun's up. I slept through the night. Good. I needed sleep. Then like a switch had been flipped, I immediately began trembling again. As fast as the peace came to me last night, it was removed. I thought, Oh no... here we go again. What in the world is happening? I began calling out to God again, "Oh God, I need your help. Please help me. I don't know what's going on... please help me." Then the name of my aunt who lives in California came to my mind: "Call Abigail." I thought, hey, that's a good idea. And I got up and called my friend, Kelly. That's right, Kelly. I can be stubborn.

We began talking, and I filled her in, and she said, "Nicole, you need to go see my therapist. She has helped me tremendously." But this helping that she received and referred to made her a self-centered person who always looked out for number one. I know there are good therapists out there, but I watched my friend become a harsh person. She was out to fulfill herself first—in all things. I knew seeing her therapist was not the answer. But to be polite, I got the name and number of her therapist and thanked my friend, and got off the phone. Then I heard again, "Call your Aunt Abigail." Once more, I thought, that's a good idea. So I picked up the phone and called my Aunt Christie.

I quickly filled her in, and she suggested that I get the same prescription she had been prescribed. She went on touting how much it helped her anxieties. I knew instantly that this was not the answer, but I graciously listened to her since I initiated the phone call. She recommended her doctor, and again, to be polite, I took the information and thanked her. I hung up, and again it came, "Call your Aunt Abigail," and again I thought, that's a good idea. I picked up the phone and called my Aunt Abigail.

"Hello," she said.

"Abigail, this is Nicole."

"Nicole? It's so good to hear from you. What's going on in your neck of the woods?"

"Oh Abigail, I need to talk with you." I began filling her in on things, and immediately she said, "Honey, you're under conviction. God's calling you to himself." Everything within me resonated with this as truth. A well of tears gushed forth as I recognized the truth of her words. She went on, "Honey, you've been covered in a line of prayers all the way back... as far as I can remember and probably further than that."

"What do you mean?" I asked.

"Honey your great-great-grandmother prayed for all of her family-line to know Christ. She prayed for all her future generations every day of her life. Your great-grandmother, your grandmother, and aunts and uncles have prayed, too. Honey, I pray for you every day. God's calling you."

I was sobbing by now and said, "I know he is."

"Honey," she continued, "as much as you are loved by me and others, no one loves you like God does. He sent his son to pay for our sins that the way to him may be opened for us. Sin keeps us from him. Christ hung on that cross to pay for our sins so that we don't have to. He took our punishment and opened the way to God. All we have to do is accept the path God has opened—the forgiven path through Jesus Christ." I recognized this as truth as well. She then asked, "Do you want to receive Christ as your Lord and Savior today? Honey, that's simply a place of surrendering your life to him and asking him to lead you."

Crying, I said, "I don't know. You see I don't think he'll want me to

48

continue dating Brad... and I want to marry him."

She said, "Honey, he may not. But if he doesn't, he'll reveal that to you gently." I listened as she continued.

As she talked, I could see myself walking on a fence and I didn't want to get off of it. I simply wanted to keep walking the fence line. But I knew God was saying, "Decide, Nicole. Get off on one side or the other." I knew it was time for me to decide and for good this time. I knew this was my decision day... I had to decide. I had to get off the fence. I could pick which side—but I had to get off the fence.

For the first time in my life, I could understand why people drink and how easy it is to become an alcoholic. For the first time, I could see why people did drugs and how easy it is to become addicted. Here I was... God was calling me to himself. What was I going to say? He who created me was telling me that it's time to decide. Was I going to come to him or not?

How could I say no and live my life knowing that I said no to the one who created me? He was calling me to himself. Could I say no? Would I? If I did, I'd live every day knowing that I chose to live life for myself, trying to make things happen my way. I'd live knowing that I said no to God, and with that decision... peace would elude me. I knew I'd be driven to drink or to do drugs to help me forget... to forget that I turned away from the true peace of God. I'd have no peace, and I'd chase the lies that alcohol and drugs offer. I'd chase a false peace. I'd chase the lie that would destroy me. Although it would be a counterfeit peace, I'd still desire it because I'd want something to drown out the memory of saying no to God. Abigail was right. It was decision time for me. I knew it. She knew it. And I was led to call her. She was speaking truth to me, and I knew it.

I started to say yes to God, but then fear gripped me again, and I started crying. "Abigail," I said sobbing, "I'm afraid of losing Brad."

She said, "Honey, you may lose him, but God will give you peace if that happens. He will. Honey, what's happening here is the enemy is causing you to be afraid of losing him. He's trying to keep you from saying yes to God. Nicole, God is not like that. He loves you, and he'll show you his truth as you walk with him. He'll give you his peace as he leads you."

Again I recognized this as truth and said, "I know it's true. I know God's calling me to himself." I cried more, and she let me. I felt the enemy nipping at my heels. I felt his threats. They were swirling around me as if to connect with my being. The battle was raging, and my fear was great, and it was growing... but the truth she spoke that started as a faint voice was also growing greater.

I sobbed, knowing that the decision had been made; I needed to but speak it. Internally, I had already jumped off the fence, and I was standing on one side. I said, "I want to give my life to Christ." She prayed with me right then to receive Christ as my Lord and savior. And I did receive him right then and there—as my savior. The peace I desired enveloped me... I was God's child. The decision was made. When I got off the phone, I was his child, and I couldn't wait for Sunday to arrive because that's when I would go to church and declare publicly what I did on the phone with my sweet, precious Aunt Abigail.

Chapter 11

Where did That Come From?

I became a new creation! This is Christian lingo that you hear when you enter into God's family, and you identify with it right away because you feel like a new creation. Those few times in my past when I would actually meet an authentic Christian, I would wonder why there was such a difference between them and my claim to Christianity. I now know it's because I was not the real thing but now, there's no longer a difference. Those Christians from my past that I felt disconnected with, I now felt connected—even though years and miles separate us. Though I may never see them this side of heaven again, I will see them in eternity. We're in the family of God together. They are my brothers and sisters in Christ. Gone was the old Nicole. I found it strange that no one was telling me to change this or that about myself or that I needed to be different, I simply was—from the inside out.

I continued my day, doing my usual routines, but instead of trembling in unbelief, doubt, worry, and fear, I was rejoicing! I couldn't wait for Sunday to get here. That would be the day to make my declaration to Christ public, before the world... or at least all those in attendance at that little church... the same church that impacted me so many years before as a teenage girl... the same church the enemy tried to keep me from attending.

For that day, though, I continued my usual routines. After all, nothing had changed about me except my identity as God's child. I still had responsibilities and routines but being God's child made all the difference in the world. It changed my perspective on everything. How? I couldn't explain it to you if I had to, not at this point. But it had changed my perspective on being a mom, daughter, sister, friend, and girlfriend... in the best way possible.

The day passed, and the evening came. I was still basking in the joy of it all and contemplating things. I could now see the threads that connected God's calling me to himself. It actually began months ago when Chip had surgery. God's question to me then was, "Nicole, you trust me with your son's life, why don't you trust me with yours'?" I acknowledged the question but I couldn't answer it. So I pushed it aside. That's when God's wooing really manifested itself to me. He was working on my heart in spite of my ignoring him. I was too preoccupied with making my life turn out like I wanted it to, and now I could see clearly that God was connecting the dots for me. I was thankful that God loved me and interrupted my thoughts and life to get my attention. As I was contemplating it all, the phone rang. It was Brad. Oh yeah, I need to tell him. He had witnessed all those church-shopping desires and days, but now I finally get it!

"Hello."

"Hey Nicole," he said. "That was a weird ending to our night last night, huh?"

Oh yeah. I was jolted back to how it ended the night before. I remembered how eerie it was. I said, "Yeah. I really needed to get home."

"I could tell," was his response. "What's up with you?" he asked.

"Oh Brad," I said. "I finally get it."

"Get what?" he asked.

I continued, "I finally get what's been going on with me."

"Great..." he said. "Please tell me?"

I went on, "Brad, all that you said that we needed to change, you were right. But it's more. All those times of my wanting to find a church to go to and my few attempts at going here and there... they were all part of a bigger picture. Much bigger."

"What do you mean?" he asked.

"Brad, I gave my life to Christ today."

"What does that mean?" he asked.

I continued, "Brad, God was drawing me to himself. He was telling me it was time for me to decide if I would accept him or not. And today on the phone with my Aunt Abigail, I accepted Christ as my Lord and Savior." There was awkward silence. I interrupted it, "Brad, don't you see? We do need to stop drinking, we do need to get married, we do need to start going to church, but it's more than those things. God was calling me, and I had to decide."

"And it sounds like you did," he said, paused, and then continued, "What does that mean for us?"

"Brad," I said, "don't you see? Things will change for the better." There was nothing but silence on the other end. And while I expected resistance to this, I never expected what was about to transpire.

"Nicole," he said, "What the bleep is going on with you? Do you have bleep for brains?"

"What?" I was shocked.

He went on, "This all started because you know we need to stop drinking."

But I knew it was more, even before I realized it was a God thing. I realized there was more. It was the way he treated me, it was the things we did. It was the things he enjoyed. It was the things his friends enjoyed... the people, the places, and the things they enjoyed and bragged about. There were so many, many things. I could now clearly see what I couldn't distinguish or separate, earlier.

He went on: "I told you I realized we needed to stop drinking. You freaked out because I wanted to enjoy drinking for one last night. I don't get what's going on with you."

I said, "Brad, it's more. It's not just the drinking. God used those things to draw me to him. I talked with my aunt on the phone, and she knew exactly what was going on with me. I knew her words were true. God was calling me to himself, and I had to decide if I would go to him. Once I did, I could see everything so clearly. I can't wait to go to church on Sunday and make it public."

"What does that mean?" he asked.

I said, "I'll go in front of the church and let them know I accepted Jesus as Lord and Savior of my life. Then I'll get baptized."

"Baptized?" he asked. "Then what's going to happen to us?"

"What do you mean?" I asked.

"Nicole, I'm not a bleeping idiot. This is going to affect us. Our relationship will be different."

I knew there was truth in this comment. However, I hoped that it would transition well and that we'd still get married. "Brad, yes things will be different. You yourself said we need to stop drinking, and this was before God entered into the equation."

Then I heard frustration rising in his voice as he continued, "Nicole, I don't know who you think you're dealing with here. You've been brainwashed. You think God's the answer? Your life is a bleeping mess. You're a divorced woman with a child. You know how bleeping lucky you are to have me? There aren't many men who would be willing to date a woman with a child, much less marry her. And now you go and do this? You're going to end up alone. And you'll be raising Chip all bleeping alone. No one will want to marry a woman with a child much less one who has bleeping found God. You'll never marry again. Never! You think this God thing is the answer—it's the opposite. You're stupid as bleep. This is going to ruin your bleeping life. This is one of the stupidest bleeping things you've done. You need to stop this bleepity-bleep freight train while you still bleeping can. Nicole, we were good before... we just need to tweak some things. What do you say?"

I thought for a second. I couldn't get my thoughts around his words. He was so hostile towards God and me—because of God in me. The tension was enormously thick and rising. I calmly responded, "Brad, it's more than that. I don't understand everything at this point, but so much has been cleared up for me. There's a reason we're here. God made us, and he wants to be in relationship with us. I said yes to him and invited Christ into my heart and life. I want you to be happy for me."

"Happy?!?!" he was now yelling. "Nicole, what the bleepity bleep were you expecting from me? I can't believe you went and did something as bleeping stupid as this! There's no bleeping way we can stay together—now

54

you'll always be alone. Get used to it, bleep! I hope you enjoy your new bleeping relationship with God! Stupidest bleeping thing you've done. I'm so over you. You're a weak-minded person who'll come to nothing... hope you enjoy your new bleeping life! No one will be stupid enough to date you now! Good luck raising Chip all by your bleeping self. What in the bleep made you think you could do something this bleeping stupid and expect us to bleeping stay together? I'm so bleeping done with you, bleep!" He hung up the phone.

I couldn't believe it. Yet, the funny thing is that as he went on berating me, a peace came over me, a peace that I cannot explain. For some reason, this peace came to me right away and echoed this particular truth from God: "Blessed are you when you're persecuted for my sake, for great is your reward." I knew I was being persecuted for Christ's sake. How I knew this truth from God, I don't know. Perhaps I heard it on one of my church-shopping days. Doesn't matter where or how I knew it... the words came to me nonetheless. God gave me such clarity. I knew I was no longer talking to the guy I loved but to the evil one through him. There was such hate and anger over my becoming a Christian that I knew where the source was coming from, and I still had peace... the peace that had previously eluded me.

Brad had broken up with me many times before, and I was always devastated. This time, I knew God was showing me who the battle was truly with, and I had peace. He was showing me that the battle was over, that he had already won this battle, and I had peace. I knew God had it, and that he had me, and I had peace. I didn't think about it again. I went about the rest of my day, and I was never more ready for Sunday to get here.

Chapter 12

Tried by Fire

My eyes opened wide. It's Sunday! I was so excited. It was time to go to church! I looked out the window, and it was a crisp, clear, beautiful day. What I especially liked about this Sunday was that I didn't need to call my friend today. I didn't need to convince myself to go to church today. I had been eagerly waiting for today. It was here, and I was so happy! I went to church and sat on the edge of my seat listening to the pastor. Finally, he summarized the seriousness of his message and then said, "They're going to lead us in worship, and if anyone needs to come down for prayer, or to get right with God, come on down. We'll be down here for anyone who needs prayer or to talk."

The singing began, and that was my cue. I immediately went down front and to the first person that looked like he could help me. Since I was proclaiming to be a new believer, he asked me a series of questions. I guess he needed clarity to direct me. I informed him that I had already prayed to receive Christ... I was simply making a public announcement in the church. I was taken to the pastor, and when the singing stopped, he stood with me and announced to the church my declaration of faith in Christ. The church applauded my salvation, and I was so happy. Then he prayed and dismissed the church.

He then turned to me and said, "Nicole, the next step in your salvation is baptism. Christ said we're to believe and be baptized. I know it's short notice, but we're having a baptism tonight. Would you like to be baptized tonight?" My heart wanted to leap at the chance. My first thought was of course! but then I remembered what was going on at my parents' house that afternoon and evening. It was the Sunday after Thanksgiving, and my mother always celebrated Thanksgiving on that Sunday. This put less stress on her married children and allowed room for the extended family to come too. I always looked forward to seeing everyone who showed up to share the day with us. How could I explain to everyone that I was going to leave to be baptized?

I expressed some of this to the pastor, who seemed to understand and said I could get baptized another time. I paused and thought for a moment, then immediately said, "No, I want to be baptized tonight. I don't want to put this off. Nothing is more important than this. I'll be here." He told me to come an hour early to meet in his office with the others who would be baptized, and he'd explain baptism to us in more depth.

I went home, and the festivities were well underway. The aroma in the house smelled wonderful. I pulled my mother aside and told her about the baptism. I said "Chip and I'll simply sneak out and come back. Maybe no one will even notice."

She said, "Maybe?" The plan was set. Around 4:30 I grabbed Chip and we left for church.

I went to the church office and met with the pastor and three other people who were there too. The pastor explained how their church does baptisms. He explained it as if the others had seen baptisms there, and I was the only one who needed the explanation. Perhaps they had been going a while before they made their decision to follow Christ. I had no clue. The pastor said, "Once you enter the baptismal, I'll introduce you, and then you'll give a brief testimony of God's work in your life. Just tell them how God drew you to himself." I nodded like that made sense. Inside though, I was trembling like a leaf but inwardly I said to the Lord, I'll do it for you, Lord. Then he ended our time together by praying for us, and we all went to change into the clothes we brought for getting wet.

Once changed, we all lined up, and two people were in front of me. I was happy about this, since it meant I could watch and listen to examples of them sharing their stories. I listened carefully to the first person. Then the second person entered the water. From the congregation's perspective, the baptismal looked like a square cut into the wall. On the bottom, glass protruded up from the wall about two or three feet, I suppose to keep the water from spilling over. From my particular view, it looked like a rectangular pool of water. Both sides had steps that were used for getting into or out of the water, much like a pool.

The first person entered the water and walked to where the pastor was waiting in the center of the baptismal. The second person walked into the water, stopped at the top of the steps, and waited for her cue. The pastor baptized the first person and released him to exit the other side. Then he cued the second person to walk down into the baptismal. And this is where my first trial by fire began. Trial by fire is Christian terminology... it's a testing of your faith that reveals to you and to the enemy how strong your faith is.

As I watched the second person walk down the steps, a big, and I mean BIG, spider came from the side wall, and was walking across the water. Water was sloshing all directions because of the movement from our walking into the water, and because of the pastor baptizing people. I hate spiders and this was a scenario I didn't want to happen, at all! Immediately I began thinking... Hmmmmm... let's see... A big spider is now in the baptismal water and walked right where I was about to enter. And now I must enter into the same water—with the big spider. Oh sure, I can watch him while I'm at the top of the steps, but we all know what's going to happen when the second person goes under the water and comes back up. We know what's going to happen to the spider... it's going to get sloshed around, and no telling where it'll be at that point. Add to that, when I walk down into the baptismal, the water will pull in the direction I'm traveling. Then as I stand there being still while telling my story, where will the spider be? Who knows at that point!?!? BUT once I go under (to get baptized), the sloshing and pulling of the water begins all over again. My long hair will be flowing in all directions. If the spider is anywhere near my hair... yep...

we know what's going to happen. It's going to take its eight enormous legs and wrap them around my hair! Then when I'm raised up out of the water, we know the spider is catching a ride out with me and will be tangled in my hair. Oh the agony of this situation.

Now this thought process happened in just a few seconds, because my mind was racing. And I knew I had a decision to make. Was I going to face this fear? All my life I was afraid of spiders. I hated them. I studied their habits. I'm on to their trick of playing dead, and I've seen how they watch us carefully. If you're trying to catch or kill them they turn in all the same directions as you. What are they going to do? Jump on you? Sometimes they do jump. I've seen some rear up at me. Now here I was in the baptismal water with a big one. Was I going to go forward to get baptized, or was I going to say no? Would I shrink back from my Lord because of a spider? I knew the answer. It rose from within. I would not shrink back. I would enter the water come what may... I would get baptized in Christ. It was decided. I would not entertain thoughts about it again. And like clockwork, there was my cue to walk down the steps, and so I did.

Once beside the pastor, he introduced me and asked me to share a short testimonial of how I came to the Lord. I looked out and saw my son, locked eyes on him, and began to share my story.

I said, "I grew up thinking I was a Christian. Although my family quit going to church when I was about seven years old, I still thought I was a Christian because of my declaration at such a young age. Then I met a few people throughout my teenage years who were true Christians. And I thought it strange how I didn't understand them, at all. There was a big disconnect between me and them. I would think, you're a Christian and I'm a Christian but I can't relate to anything about you. After that I didn't give it much thought... I just didn't get it. When I had my son, I entrusted him to the Lord by giving him back to God. This was what my mother did with me and my siblings. She often talked to us of God, even when we quit going to Church. I knew that my son was created by God and there was no better place for him to be, than in God's hands. There was no question about that. Then my marriage ended in divorce and I eventually I started dating someone else. My life was taking a different direction than I anticipated and I wasn't happy about some of them.

Then my son needed surgery—a simple surgery—to remove both his tonsils and adenoids. As he went into surgery, I was reminded of how I gave him to the Lord at birth and there I was once again, entrusting him to the Lord's care through surgery.

"When they brought him out of recovery, I was amazed at what transpired with him and within me. He crawled off the bed and into my arms. He was dazed and confused and wanted me to hold him. I held him and didn't leave his side for the rest of the hospital stay. That night, I slept in his hospital bed with him. When he went to the bathroom, I walked with him, pulling his little I.V. stand. The following day, the doctor came to release him from the hospital. As he was going over the dos and don'ts of home care, tears began flowing down my cheeks. I couldn't stop them. They flowed like a river. Something was initiated within me. It was a questioning that began that day and led me here before you today.

"When we got home, I began going about my duties and the questioning arose again, 'If you trust your son with me,' and I knew I had entrusted him with God, 'why won't you trust me with your own life?' And I knew I didn't trust God with my life. I knew this was a paradox, and one I couldn't rectify. It's just the way it was. I didn't know why, but I determined to live with it.

"Yet as my decisions and situations continued to worsen, I would think of going to church in the distant future, and I would think that would fix things. After a period of time with this thinking and lifestyle, a woman asked me if I wanted to receive Christ as Lord and Savior, and I said no. I wanted to marry my boyfriend, and I imagined God would not want me to do that. Later I asked God to keep me alive until I figured things out, and he did. But he put me under serious conviction and told me to choose. And I did. I chose him. Nothing else mattered but being right with him. Now I ask for him to fill me with his wisdom, knowledge, and understanding. And I'm here tonight to declare to all that I am his."

At this moment, one I'll never forget, the pastor said, "I find it interesting that Nicole is asking God to fill her with his wisdom, knowledge, and understanding."

And I thought, why wouldn't I? And I think it's strange that you think that's strange! Shouldn't that be the prayer of all Christians? He prayed for me and then baptized me. Under I went, in the likeness of Christ in his death, and up I came, in the likeness of his resurrected life! The old had gone, and the new had come. I was a new creation in Christ!!! And I would be forever his!!! And I never once thought about that stinking spider.

I got dressed and stayed for the service, and then we went home to rejoin my family. I was surprised that there was no opposition or disappointment. In fact, my father called me to himself and said, "Nicole, Mom told me about what you did tonight. I'm proud of you." And he just looked at me.

I said, "Thanks," and he just kept looking at me. I interrupted the awkwardness by telling Chip he needed to get ready for bed.

The next few days were uneventful. I didn't hear from Brad, but I was not concerned about it. I was excited about my new life as a Christian. Then a few days later, he called. He wanted to understand why I decided to become a Christian. He wanted me back, and he let me know that. I knew I needed counsel and that we should talk to someone in the church. I needed help to navigate our relationship because things needed to be different. He argued with me at first and then acquiesced. I called the singles pastor, Kevin, and filled him in on things. He said he would call Brad and meet with him. I was happy someone was entering in to help me in this area. I knew I loved Brad, but our relationship needed God in it.

Brad met with Kevin a few times, and he became a Christian! How great was that? Kevin counseled that we should take three months apart and grow in our individual walks with God so that when we came back together, we could be strong in God. We both saw the wisdom in that. I was so happy for Brad and for our relationship. Kevin counseled that we not even talk on the phone. We just needed to grow in our walks with God. We agreed, and I couldn't have been happier.

A week went by, and I could only imagine the growth that was taking place with Brad, because I was growing so much. Then he called. I was shocked. He said, "Nicole, I know I'm going against the rules, but I miss you so much. I had to hear your voice."

I said, "Oh Brad, I miss you too. And it's good to hear your voice too. How's it been going?"

We had a good conversation, and then he asked, "Why can't we see each other? Why can't we grow together?"

I said, "I don't know, that's just what Kevin suggested."

He said, "Who is Kevin? I mean, who is he to make us alter our lives according to what he says?"

"Brad..." I began, but he interrupted. "Nicole... hear me out. I know we can't be like we used to be, but to stay apart for three months? For what good reason? Maybe he likes you and wants you to get over me. Ever think about that?"

"Brad... that's not it."

"How do you know? You're a good-looking girl. Not many good-looking girls probably come into his church world."

"Brad... that's not it."

He continued, "Then give me one good reason why we can't grow in God together?"

I couldn't. My head and heart were reeling. What he was asking for was a good thing; to be able to grow together in our new lives with God. This was what I wanted, and Brad knew that. He began arguing from that perspective.

"Nicole, before you got saved, you knew things needed to be different. You became a Christian first, and then I did too. Now that we're both Christians, why can't we grow in our new lives together? It makes no sense to put that off because some guy at the church says we should. And again, he may have ulterior motives for suggesting that. As he keeps you away from me, he can move in closer to you."

"Brad, that's not it, and you know it."

"Then what is it? We love each other Nicole. Why would God want us to stay apart now that we're with him?"

I said, "I just think we need to get Kevin's thoughts on it. Let's call him."

He interrupted, "Nicole, did you join a cult?"

I abruptly said, "What?!? You know better! Why would you ask that? Brad, I don't understand this."

"Nicole, you should be able to make a decision on your own. Who says Kevin's right and we're wrong?"

I said, "Well, he's been a Christian longer, and all he's suggesting is that we take a three-month separation to grow in our individual walks with God. Then we'll be strong enough to pick our relationship back up."

He said, "Unless he wants to get three months between us so he can make his move on you. I've seen this kind of thing hundreds of times. You know it happens! Why can't we grow together? I love you, and you love me. We both can grow in the Lord together. Why can't we?"

I didn't have an answer, and my heart was being pulled. This was what I always wanted. However, before, I thought I'd have to marry him before I could get him into church. And now here we both are, Christians. And he wants to grow together. I didn't have strong enough answers to say no, to say no to him or to my heart. "Okay Brad, you may be right. I do love you, and God knows that we love each other. After all we've been through surely he's for us if he's now in it with us. I think we can see each other and grow together."

He breathed a sigh of relief. "Nicole, I love you. We'll be fine. I'm just happy we can see each other again. Can we see each other tonight?"

I hesitated but had no reason to say no. "Sure. Want to have dinner?"

He said, "Yes, I'll pick you up at 6:30. I love you, Nicole."

"I love you too, Brad. I'll see you tonight." And we hung up.

I had an uneasy feeling, but I couldn't reconcile my feelings with my thoughts, so I felt I should move forward. I prayed God was in it, since I was counting on his being in it. After all, I did love Brad. We had already slept together, and didn't that mean God really wanted us to stay together? I wasn't certain of anything but felt God would want us to stay together since he hates divorce... I mean... in his eyes, we were kind of married. Right? I didn't have hard answers. But now that God was in it, I would move forward in our love for each other while looking to God.

The journey to my salvation was long and varied. I guess you could say I was stubborn about things and wanted them my way. I'm thankful that God is patient, and I know he'll help me in my walk. Are Brad and I supposed to go against Kevin's guidance and navigate our relationship on our own? I don't know. Time will tell, and God will lead. I know he will. I'm hopeful, and I'll trust in him.

Only the beginning...

More titles from Kayla...

Discussion Book SERIES — BOOK 2
Dying Is Part of This World
Kayla Jarmon
ILLUSTRATED BY PIPER MIRU

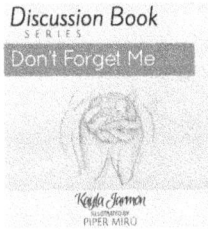

Discussion Book SERIES
Don't Forget Me
Kayla Jarmon
ILLUSTRATED BY PIPER MIRU

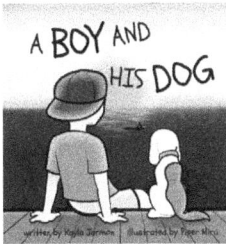

A BOY AND HIS DOG
Written by Kayla Jarmon | Illustrated by Piper Miru

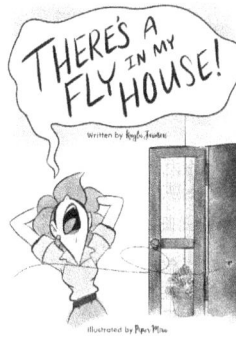

THERE'S A FLY IN MY HOUSE!
Written by Kayla Jarmon
Illustrated by Piper Miru

A Christmas JOURNEY
Written by Kayla Jarmon
Illustrated by Piper Miru

Oh No! My Cat Lost Her Cat Skills!
By Kayla Jarmon

...and more to come!

For these titles and more, please visit
kaylajarmon.com